MOHAMED SALAH

THE ULTIMATE FAN BOOK

Adrian Besley

CARLTON
BOOKS

CONTENTS

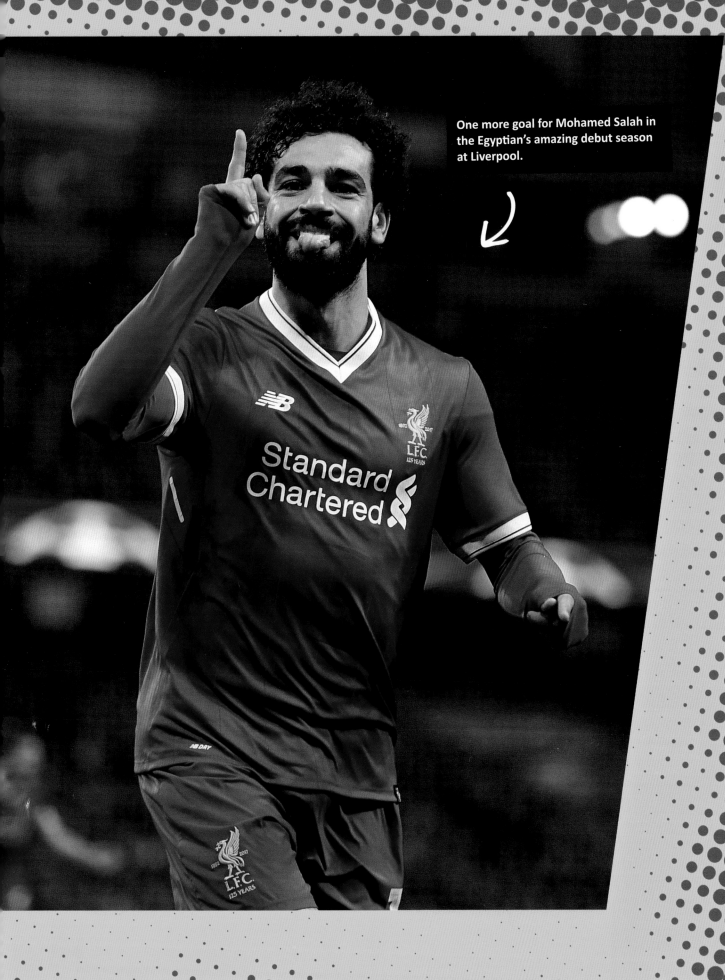

One more goal for Mohamed Salah in the Egyptian's amazing debut season at Liverpool.

INTRODUCTION

It's 2018 and Liverpool FC have a new hero to follow in the footsteps of Kevin Keegan, Kenny Dalglish, Steven Gerrard and Luis Suárez. They call him "The Egyptian King", but on the teamsheet he's listed as Mohamed Salah – and that name is enough to strike fear into any opposition.

Salah's 2017–18 season was breathtaking. From his debut goal – a brave goal-line tap-in against Watford – he kept scoring; a jinking run, an audacious chip, a cracking volley and other glorious goals adding to the trademark one-on-one finishes. By the end of the season he had amassed 32 Premier League goals and had inspired Liverpool to a thrilling run to the Champions League Final.

Some called his £36.8 million transfer a gamble, but not those who had seen him torment defences for Roma, or those who had begged him to stay after a short but memorable half-season at Fiorentina. Even those at his first European club, Basel, had great memories of the flying Egyptian. Only in an unhappy season at Chelsea had he failed to impress. At all these clubs he had learned from

great coaches, listened to experienced players and put in hours of practice to improve his already prodigious natural talent.

Humble and modest, Salah plays the game with a smile on his face and he is loved by fans around the world. But nowhere is he treasured more than in the country of his birth, Egypt. They have watched the skinny teenage winger at the unfashionable Cairo club El Mokawloon develop into one of the world's best. They are proud that he represents Egypt and the Muslim faith in Europe; they are honoured that he retains such a strong connection with his home country and they are thrilled that he has inspired them to reach their first World Cup since 1990.

To see an injured and tearful Mo Salah leave the Champions League Final so early was a sad sight for any football fan. But, as we trace his journey from schoolboy to star and discover the quiet and determined man away from the spotlight, it is clear that there are many more magic moments, goals and smiles still to come from the Egyptian King.

Mo took Roberto Firmino's No.11 squad number at Liverpool as the Brazilian moved to No.9.

Salah's exciting play soon made him a firm favourite at Anfield.

THE YOUNG MOHAMED SALAH

In the small Egyptian town of Nagrig, the children kicking the ball around have one dream: they want to emulate the man they call "the Happiness Maker": Mohamed Salah, Liverpool's top scorer and Africa's top footballer.

Nagrig, a farming village 80 miles north-west of Cairo, looks much like any other small Egyptian town. Alfalfa and wheat fields surround the dusty main road and the quiet narrow streets and alleys full of unpainted houses. However, Nagrig has an all-weather pitch, new school buildings, a recently built community centre and land marked out for a vital treatment works to supply fresh water – all courtesy of a famous son plying his trade 6,000 miles away.

For the whole of Egypt, Mo Salah is a footballing idol, but for the population of Nagrig he is more than this. Salah was born here on 15 June 1996, growing up and playing with them or their children. They watch his displays for club and country with pride. For Salah has never forgotten his roots, returning regularly and providing much-needed resources for the many impoverished inhabitants. It is no wonder that they have a special name for him: "the Happiness Maker".

Salah inherited his love of football from his father and uncles, who played in the village's local amateur team through the 1980s and 1990s. When he wasn't playing, the young Salah was watching football on television. He loved the Champions League, especially the players with magic in their feet like Ronaldo (the Brazilian), Zidane and Totti.

By the time he was eight years old, his father and a local coach had noticed that Mo's speed and talent marked him out among the enthusiastic young boys. The others just couldn't get the ball off him. Four years later, Mo's father took the prodigy to join his first real team, Ittihad Basyoun, located in the nearest city, a 30-minute bus ride away. He wasn't there long.

The story told locally is that a scout came to watch another lad but was blown away by Salah's skills. In 2006, Mo was invited to join a team in Tanta; it was a 90-minute bus journey, but it was a huge step forward. The team was run by El-Mokawloon, an Egyptian Premier League club based in Cairo.

Mo often returns to his hometown of Nagrig in Egypt and makes some dreams come true.

The mural on the wall of the Youth Centre is just one sign of Nagrig residents' pride in their favourite son.

The Mohamed Ayyad Al-Tantawy school boasts a fine all-weather football pitch, paid for by their most famous former pupil.

TURNING PRO AT EL MOKAWLOON

Mo Salah's began life at his first professional club as a full-back. But given an opportunity, the teenager with lightning pace and the ability to take chances coolly was soon getting noticed...

El Mokawloon (the "Arab Contractors") are a well-known club in Cairo, Egypt. Often in the shadow of city giants Al Alhy and Zamalek, they look back to the 1980s and 90s for their glory days, but nevertheless they have maintained a position in Egyptian football's top flight since 2005. For a quiet 14-year-old fast-tracked to the club in the big city, it was an ideal start.

Mo Salah had never shone in his academic studies, and now he was only spending two hours a day at school, leaving at 11.00 to begin a four-hour journey on four or five buses. He would train until six in the evening before making the same journey home. At least he had plenty of time to read his school books!

On the pitch, Mo was making his name as a dynamic left-back. He would often dribble through the whole opposition but invariably squandered the final opportunity. The coach Said El-Shishini claims that after a game in which El Mokawloon won 4–0, Mo was in tears after missing five chances. It was then he decided to switch him to right wing. By the end of the season, Salah had notched 35 goals.

In May 2010, at the age of just 16, he made his debut for the senior team, coming on as a substitute in a 1–1 draw with El Mansoura. He began to establish himself in the following season, scoring his first goal in a cup game at Suez Club with a sublime left foot outstep finish.

By the 2011–12 season, Salah was a regular, scoring seven times in 15 games in a struggling team. Mostly he sprinted away to beat keepers in a one-on-one, but against Al-Ittihad he dribbled from his own half before sliding the ball past the goalie. Tragically, that season was curtailed after a riot, following a match between Al-Masry and Al-Ahly, led to the death of 74 people, but the young Salah had done enough to turn heads...

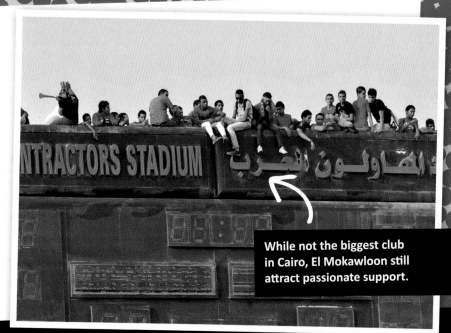

While not the biggest club in Cairo, El Mokawloon still attract passionate support.

The 35,000 capacity Arab Contractors Stadium, home to Mo's first professional club, El Mokawloon.

BASEL – THE SWISS FINISHING SCHOOL

For a teenaged Egyptian in Switzerland life was never going to be easy. But with application, attention and talent, Salah went from "Chance Killer" to lethal weapon.

Salah's displays for El Mokawloon had drawn attention from Egypt's big clubs and even from Premier League clubs Hull City and Stoke City, but Swiss champions FC Basel were ahead of the game. They had received favourable words on the skinny Egyptian winger in the FIFA Under-20 World Cup and as Egypt prepared for the 2012 Olympics, they arranged a friendly to see him in action.

"I will never forget what I saw that day," Basel president Bernhard Heusler told Sky Sports. "He only played the second half but I had never seen a player with so much speed in my entire life." Within a month they had struck the deal.

Still only 19, Mo had a difficult time settling in to a strange country. His speed was obvious for all to see, but in front of goal his usual composure was

Salah's strike against Tottenham Hotspur took Basel to a UEFA Europa League quarter-final in 2013.

missing. Though he missed enough to earn the nickname "Chance Killer", his coaches were not concerned; Mo was willing to work hard.

Swiss striker Alexander Frei told *World Soccer* magazine: "There wasn't much in the way of pattern to his play. I put him on special shooting sessions and it did make him more effective in front of goal."

Salah's form gradually improved. Basel went on to win another championship, and in the UEFA Europa League, his goal helped beat Tottenham in the quarter-finals and he found the net again in a defeat to Chelsea in the semis.

The next season saw Salah step up another level, setting up goals for his strikers and scoring five himself as Basel began an undefeated run that took them to the top of the table. In December he was named Swiss Player of the Year, his two virtuoso performances against Chelsea in the Champions League raising Mo's profile once again. He scored in both ties and his mesmerizing footwork in the first game left the England full-back Ashley Cole dizzy.

The previous year, Basel coach Murat Yakin had joked: "If Mohamed could score as well, he would not be here any more." He was about to be proved right.

Salah took his time settling in at Basel, but in his second season there, he was named Swiss Player of the Year.

Mo's impressive displays against Chelsea in the UEFA Champions League in 2013 helped bring him to the attention of the London club.

EGYPTIAN GOD

Mo Salah has already established himself as the greatest ever Egyptian footballer. In his homeland he offers something more than that: hope. His humble story has given heart to millions across the African continent.

It is 8 October 2017, in Alexandria, Egypt, and 100,000 fans stand silent and tense as Mo Salah prepares to take a penalty. Egypt are drawing with Congo in a World Cup qualifier they must win to secure their first World Cup finals place for 28 years. Four minutes after the 90 have elapsed, Salah has the chance to win the game. Calmly the 25-year-old strides up to the ball and slams it to the right of the keeper. In the stadium the fans go crazy. Outside, joyous pandemonium breaks out throughout the country.

After celebrating with his teammates, Salah sank to the ground in prayer. Already the talisman of an improving national team, that penalty made a national hero of the striker and confirmed his place as the nation's greatest ever player.

Now every coffee shop has a Salah poster, his image covers Ramadan lanterns and foodstuffs and Egyptians – some of them former Manchester United supporters – buy Liverpool shirts with his name in Arabic. It was even reported that in the 2018 presidential elections, up to one million people crossed out the two candidates' names and wrote in Salah's instead.

For his part, Mo has never forgotten his homeland. His charity donations are legendary; when offered a luxury villa as a reward for the World Cup qualification, he politely refused and requested a donation be made to his home village instead. He took the number 74 shirt at Fiorentina to pay tribute to the Port Said Stadium victims and when the government desperately needed funds to prop up the economy, Salah reportedly donated £210,000 of his own money.

To many in Egypt, Mo Salah offers something more than football. As the country struggles with political turmoil and economic instability, Mo's determination, strong religious faith and humble demeanour show how even a boy from the smallest village can be successful. He has become an inspiration for children in Egypt and across Africa. When Salah won the African Player of the Year award in 2018, he addressed them directly in his acceptance speech, with the message: "Never stop dreaming, never stop believing."

Fans of The Pharaohs – Egypt's national side – celebrate their star player and hero.

Ahmed Fathy's huge mural in downtown Cairo is evidence of Salah's place as a national icon.

15

CHELSEA BLUES

A big money move to Premier League title chasers Chelsea presented Mohamed Salah with a chance to perform on the big stage. But somehow, it all went wrong.

Hopeful. Mo Salah arrives at Stamford Bridge for a new chapter in his career.

impact in the Premier League.

He didn't feature again for more than a month, until he came on as a substitute against Arsenal. After just four minutes on the pitch, he slotted a trademark finish past Wojciech Szczesny, the last in a six-goal rout. He had opened his Chelsea account. When, in April, he marked his first start with a man-of-the-match performance and a goal against Stoke City, Blues fans settled in to see what their much-hyped signing could do.

In late January 2014, Liverpool were poised to add the pace and skills of Mo Salah to their title-chasing squad. A £12 million deal had been arranged with Basel when the Anfield club received a surprise email from Switzerland: Salah had decided to join Chelsea.

"First of all, he won't score against Chelsea," joked the Blues' boss Jose Mourinho. Many soon wondered if that really was Chelsea's motivation.

Salah arrived at Stamford Bridge on 27 January 2014 for a £16 million fee, taking the No. 15 shirt. Joining an exciting line-up alongside André Schürrle, Eden Hazard, Oscar and Willian, it was no surprise to see Salah begin his Chelsea career on the bench.

However those who had seen his Champions League displays were taken aback when, after a few substitute appearances, Mourinho declared that the 21-year-old was not ready to make an

All smiles. Mo Salah and Chelsea manager Jose Mourinho share a joke during training.

Salah kept his place for Chelsea's victory at Anfield which dented Liverpool's title hopes but in that game, and in others, he under-performed and was regularly substituted. Hauled off at half-time in the penultimate game of the season against Norwich, he was reportedly in tears in the dressing room.

Never one to give up without a fight, Salah worked hard in training and in the gym.

He enjoyed a good pre-season, but as the campaign got underway, he found himself the least favoured of a talented strike-force. By January, Mo had made just three league starts and, after he was substituted during an embarrassing FA Cup defeat to Bradford, matters came to a head.

Eight days later he found himself in Italy...

Frustrated. Mo's Chelsea career failed to take off as he found himself sidelined and out of form.

A fresh start. Mo arrives for a loan spell at Fiorentina. Few expected him to impress quite so quickly.

PURPLE PATCH

If ever a player has hit the ground running at a new club, it was Mo Salah. In just six months on loan at Fiorentina, he turned around his career and became the most wanted man in Italy.

Salah was in good company at Fiorentina where, in January 2015, he went on loan from Chelsea for the remainder of the 2014–15 season. La Viola had made a habit of picking up Premier League misfits with Micah Richards, Marcos Alonso, Alberto Aquilani and David Pizarro all rejuvenating their careers in Florence as the team re-established itself as a top Serie A club.

From the moment he set foot in Italy, Mo came alive. After an impressive 25-minute debut against Atalanta, he started against Sassuolo, creating one goal and scoring another. He then went on to score six times in as many games, including a goal in the Europa League as Fiorentina knocked out Spurs, and a prized winner against Inter Milan.

He was the talk of Serie A, already being compared to club legends such as Rui Costa, Gabriel Batistuta and even Roberto Baggio. When Salah went on a 60-yard Maradona-style dribble

Salah's second goal against Juventus in the Coppa Italia semi-final condemned Juventus to their first home defeat in 48 matches.

to strike against Juventus, the newcomer became the team's top scorer. Of course, the fans loved him, serenading him with choruses of: *"Siam venuti fin qua per veder segnare Salah"* ("We came here to see Salah score").

It was a complete reversal of his time at Chelsea as Salah adapted to life not only in Italy but also on the pitch. He played as a winger in a 4–3–3 formation, but also as a striker alongside Mario Gomez. He scored more goals against Sampdoria, Empoli and Parma, and helped Fiorentina to reached the semi-finals of the Europa League and a fourth-place finish in Serie A. In Florence, expectations were high for the 2015–16 season.

When Salah's loan was arranged, it was understood to be an 18-month deal in which Fiorentina's star, Juan Cuadrado, moved permanently to Chelsea. However, the impact Mo made in just six months tempted richer Serie A clubs. Fiorentina were desperate to keep their new star, offering him increased financial incentives, but Mo was in demand and bigger and better clubs were in the chase.

Salah's superb performances in purple left everyone at Fiorentina desperate to hang on to their loan star.

WHEN IN ROME

Salah's two-season sojourn at Roma saw him develop into an intelligent and scintillating forward. While the club failed to win trophies, their young star was gaining admirers in Italy and abroad.

"I chose Roma for many reasons. I want to win something here. I like the city. I like the club." This was Mo's explanation as to why he chose Roma from his Italian suitors. It was, initially, a loan deal from Chelsea for £5 million, but with an option to complete the deal for another £15 million. Greeted at Fiumicino Airport by hundreds of fans, there was pressure on the 23-year-old to perform. He did not disappoint.

With blistering acceleration and clever movement, Salah fitted into coach Rudi Garcia's team. After a stuttering start Roma clicked. Salah's first goal came in his fourth match, a scintillating left-foot 20-yard volley, and he was soon creating chances for Miralem Pjanic and Diego Perotti.

At the end of October, he returned to Fiorentina with his new team. In front of a crowd still bitter at his departure, Salah scored a brilliant goal (and was later dismissed after a second yellow card) as a 2–1 victory saw Roma replace his former side at the top of Serie A.

Unfortunately, an ankle injury left Salah sidelined for a month and Roma's form dipped. In the New Year, they replaced Garcia with Luciano Spalletti. Despite the new coach's attacking philosophy (Roma finished third but were top scorers) Mo credits Spalletti with improving his game tactically and defensively. And he kept scoring. He doubled his previous season's count with 14 goals and six assists in 34 appearances and was voted the club's Player of the Season.

In the next season, Salah made his move permanent and continued to improve. He scored 15 league goals (including his first ever hat-trick, against Bologna in November) and recorded 11 assists. His game had taken another step up: not only were his touch and control more assured but so were his positional awareness and attacking instincts. Still, the *Scudetto* proved elusive again as Roma finished runners-up behind Juventus.

One more season with Salah might have been enough to push for the title, but financial pressures were growing. As Roma readied themselves for offers for their star man, an old admirer was taking an interest.

Salah's understated goal celebration was becoming a common sight in Serie A.

Mo's speed and movement were key factors to his success at Roma, but importantly he also developed his defensive play.

MO SALAH AT HOME

Family, faith and Playstation keep Mo happy as he settles down to life in Liverpool – although he still finds the accent difficult to understand!

Mo Salah loves his fast cars but he's a family man who likes the quiet life.

After the final whistle sounded for Liverpool's final match of the 2017–18 season, a 4–0 victory over Brighton, Mo Salah was presented with the Golden Boot as the Premier League's top scorer. Joining him on the pitch were his wife Magi and daughter Makkah.

Salah leads a very private life, but the Anfield crowd clearly enjoyed sharing their love for the player with his family. They especially enjoyed watching three-year-old Makkah displaying her football skills on the hallowed turf.

Magi and Mo met as teenagers at school and they married in his hometown of Nagrig in December, 2013. According to reports, there were thousands present and famous Egyptian singers and actors Hamada Helal, Abdel Baset Hamouda and Saad Al Sughayar – the latter famous for his song *"Hatgawiz"* ("I'm Getting Married") – all sang at the wedding.

Mo is a quiet family man who likes to stay in reading, watching TV or playing his favourite sport – football – on his Playstation! He's been playing since he was a child, where he'd pick Liverpool as his team, and now even admits that when he plays Salah in the game, he's better than the real-life version. He's doing his best to pick up the local Scouse dialect but admitted to the club website: "The accent is so hard to understand. Flanno's [full-back Jon Flanagan's] accent is the worst one – I cannot understand anything from him."

Though Mo Salah has the usual footballer's trappings of a beautiful house and a garage full of supercars, his deep connection with his home country and his faith mark him out from many other players. He makes numerous return trips to Egypt and his charity donations are well documented. Even in Liverpool, he frequents a restaurant owned by an Egyptian for his favourite hummus falafel.

Mo is a devout Muslim. This plays an important part in many aspects of his life but is publicly demonstrated each time he scores. After hugging his teammates, he raises his hands to the heavens and kneels to pray. It is a goal celebration which has, thankfully, been respected by much-maligned football fans across Europe – just one more delight brought to us by the "Egyptian King".

Salah's trademark goal celebration is now a familiar sight to the Liverpool faithful.

MOHAMED SALAH'S SUPER SKILLS

Pace and balance always marked Mo out as a stunning talent, but expert coaching and hard work have seen him develop the skills that set him apart as a world class striker.

Lightning-fast pace has always been a feature of Salah's game – with and without the ball.

FINISHING

There are two classic Salah finishes: he out-paces defenders to calmly slot the ball past the keeper or he cuts in from right to left and curls it into the far corner. He is also capable of dinking the ball over the goalkeeper, stunning volleys, precision shooting through defences and even headers. Finishing is something Mo has had to work on: "If he was more clinical, his value would have another zero!" Bernhard Heusler, President of FC Basel when Mo was there, once joked.

PURE SPEED

Mo is fast. Deadly fast. With or without the ball, Salah can out-sprint most defenders. But speed on its own is not enough: anticipating a pass, choosing whether to run inside or outside of a defender and thinking while on the move are all attributes Mo developed in Italy.

Deft touches and unerring power make Mo's left foot a deadly and precise weapon.

MAGIC LEFT FOOT

"Once he adapted and developed that left foot, he was always going to have a big career," remarked former Liverpool player, Philipp Degen, a teammate of Mo at Basel. Now, with both wielding a magic wand of a left foot, Mo has been compared to the world's best, Leo Messi. They share an amazing ability to control and manipulate the ball and to shoot with the inside or outside of the foot.

VERSATILITY

In his younger days Mo was known for his direct style, using his speed to take him past defenders. In Italy however, he was taught to play both wide and in the centre, even dropping deeper. He learned how to play off other strikers and bring his teammates into play. At Liverpool, Klopp has utilized all these skills, deploying him in different attacking positions.

A familiar sight as Mo leaves defenders in his wake on another mazy dribble.

DRIBBLING

Salah's four-goal haul against Watford in 2018 led Liverpool boss Jürgen Klopp to compare him to the great Diego Maradona. His dribbling skills certainly bear comparison. Hard work in the gym has added strength to the Egyptian's armoury. Combined with great control and superb balance, he has the ability to twist and turn his way through defence-packed penalty areas.

GREAT ROMA GOALS

Fiorentina might have made Salah a better player, but at Roma he became a superb finisher. In his 65 games for the *giallorossi* he scored 29 goals, including a fair few gems.

ROMA V BAYER LEVERKUSEN, 4 November 2015

The Champions League tie was little more than a minute old when Mo collected the ball outside his own penalty area. He passed to Edin Dzeko on the halfway line, who turned and knocked a beautiful pass into the Leverkusen half and the path of the speeding Salah. Mo still had work to do. Out-pacing the defence, he coolly stroked the ball past the keeper. It was Roma's fastest ever Champions League goal and just nine seconds elapsed between Salah collecting the ball and scoring.

Despite sprinting more than half the length of the pitch Mo has energy to celebrate his sensational goal against Bayer Leverkusen.

ROMA V PALERMO, 21 February 2016

Mo had just put Roma 3–0 up in the game, but he clearly wasn't in the mood to let up. Having miscontrolled a through ball with his chest, Salah gave the Palermo keeper a chance to push the ball away. Regaining possession, he found himself on the by-line with the goalkeeper and a defender between him and the goal. His chip seemed to defy physics, the ball going between the two and bouncing into an open goal. Truly astonishing.

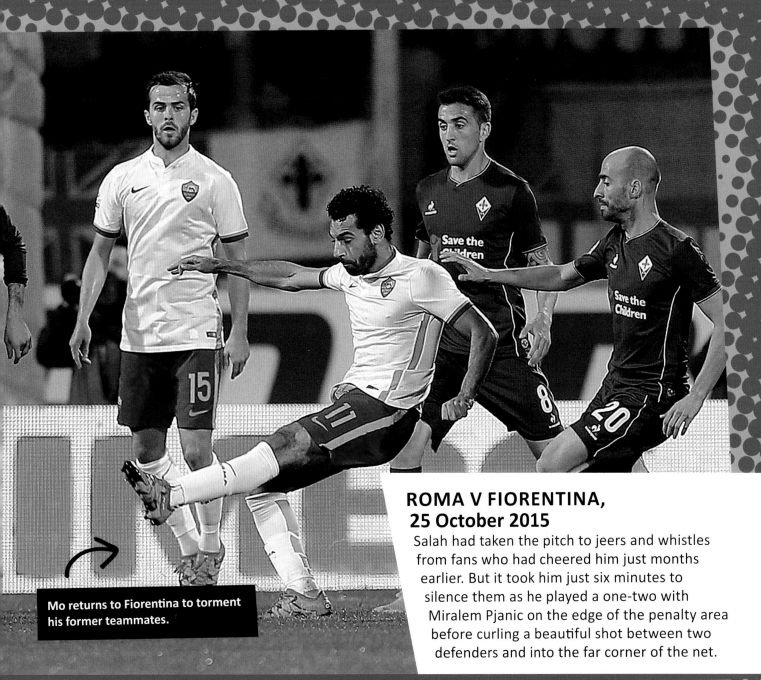

Mo returns to Fiorentina to torment his former teammates.

ROMA V FIORENTINA, 25 October 2015

Salah had taken the pitch to jeers and whistles from fans who had cheered him just months earlier. But it took him just six minutes to silence them as he played a one-two with Miralem Pjanic on the edge of the penalty area before curling a beautiful shot between two defenders and into the far corner of the net.

ROMA V SASSUOLO, 20 September 2015

Mo Salah had impressed in his early appearances but it wasn't until his fourth match that he made it onto the scoresheet. It was worth waiting for. As a looping header cleared the ball from a corner, Mo was 30 yards from goal. He waited for the ball to drop before timing a ferocious volley hard and low into the left corner of the net. What a way to endear yourself to your new fans!

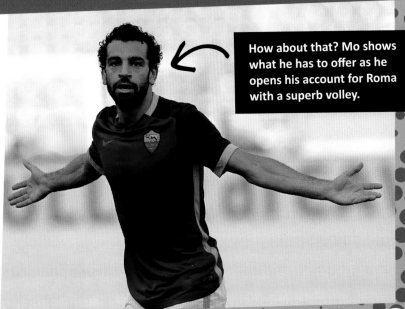

How about that? Mo shows what he has to offer as he opens his account for Roma with a superb volley.

Wherever he has played, Mo has been a popular member of the squad.

TRAINING WITH MO

Throughout Mo Salah's career, in the good times and periods of frustration, one thing is clear. He never stops working to improve his game.

Liverpool teammate Trent Alexander-Arnold tells a story about Mo Salah's first day at pre-season training with the Reds. The England full-back tells of an exercise where the players just carry on running laps faster and faster until they are too exhausted to continue. One by one they dropped out until it was just him and Mo. And then it was just Mo, but the new signing didn't stop; he kept going and going. That's how the Liverpool players discovered the determination and fitness of their new teammate.

Those who played and coached Mo through his career wouldn't have been surprised by the story. His work-rate and application in training were features at every one of his clubs. All his coaches speak of his willingness to stay behind after the rest of the team had departed to work on a facet of his game.

In the early years he worked on his finishing. He would be visibly upset when he missed chances – even when his team won – and in the national team, at Basel and even in Italy, coaches told how it motivated him to work even harder. Bob Bradley, who coached Mo in Egypt's national tem, recalled: "He wanted to work on his finishing. When you showed him things in training, the next day you'd see him doing it without even thinking about it."

His willingness to put in extra hours at the training ground marks Mo out as a dedicated professional.

Mo's Liverpool teammates are regularly astonished by the audacious skills he displays in training sessions.

Italian football required him to work on other disciplines. Gym work enabled him to become more muscular and stronger on the ball and he credits Roma boss Luciano Spalletti with spending the time with him in training to develop his tactical knowledge and his defensive acumen. And at Liverpool, where he often dazzles teammates with his skills in training, it has been noted that he is still doing extra work outside of the group sessions.

Reds skipper Jordan Henderson said, "He's always doing work behind the scenes, always in the gym doing little bits here and there and working on his shooting and stuff in training."

That's Mo, Golden Boot winner, PFA Player of the Year — and still not satisfied.

PRINCE OF EGYPT

Long before Liverpool supporters had dubbed him "The Egyptian King", Mo Salah was already the star of the national team.

Mo first gained international tournament experience in 2011, playing in the 2011 African Youth Championships in South Africa and the 2011 FIFA Under-20 World Cup in Colombia. On 3 September that year, he made his senior international debut in a 2–1 away defeat to Sierra Leone, but kept his place against Niger a month later, when he scored his first international goal.

For a nation unused to international success, Egypt's journey to the quarter-finals of the London 2012 Olympic Games captured the public's attention. It was a campaign largely inspired by Mo Salah, who scored in every group game and was rewarded with the African football confederation's prestigious CAF Most Promising Talent of the Year award.

It gave Egypt high hopes for qualifying for the 2014 World Cup in Brazil. Mo hit six goals in the group stage, including his first international hat-trick against Zimbabwe. It brought his tally to 15 goals in just 21 appearances. He scored the only goal in Mozambique to leave Egypt a two-legged final qualification round away from a World Cup place. Unfortunately Mo was helpless as a top-quality Ghana team trounced them 6–1 in the first leg.

Egypt hadn't qualified for the African Cup of Nations qualifiers since 2010, but Salah's 90th-minute equalizer in the away tie with key opponents Nigeria gave them a chance of reaching the 2017 tournament. In the return fixture, Ramadan Sobhi netted the only goal, set up by Mo's charged-down cheeky back-flick. Egypt were on their way to the Gabon finals.

Salah had scored four times in that qualifying run and three more in the 2018 World Cup qualifiers. In a must-win tie against Congo in October 2017, he typically burst through from the wing to put Egypt ahead.

However, an 88th-minute equalizer put their World Cup finals place in jeopardy but, with just seconds remaining, a clumsy challenge saw Egypt awarded a penalty. With ultimate coolness, Salah stepped up and – as the whole of the country watched – hammered it home. Now he really was the King of Egypt...

Salah was only 20 when he helped Egypt to reach the quarter-finals of the London 2012 Olympic Games.

Mo impressed the watching Basel scouts with his displays in the 2011 Under-20 World Cup in Colombia.

Mo is carried off on the shoulders of teammates after his last-gasp penalty sent Egypt to the 2018 World Cup finals.

MO SALAH STATS

Goals, assists, records, awards... Mo just keeps adding to his. Here are some of the numbers that mark out the career of the Egyptian King.

3 Mo is the first man to win three Premier League Player of the Month awards in a season, in November 2017, February and March 2018.

7 In an amazing run, Mo Salah scored in seven consecutive matches, from an FA Cup tie against West Bromwich on 27 January 2018 to a Premier League win over Newcastle United on 3 March.

17 The number of Premier League clubs Mo scored against in 2017–18. No player has ever scored against more teams in one season.

32 When he scored against Brighton & Hove Albion on the final day of the Premier League season, Mohamed clinched the Golden Boot and set a new single-season goalscoring record for the League since it started in 1992–93.

18 million Mo's combined following on Instagram, Twitter and Facebook.

57

The number of minutes it took for Mohamed Salah to open his account in his Liverpool debut against Watford in August 2017.

44

Mo's goal tally across all competitions in 2017-18. No Liverpool player has scored more in their Premier League debut season.

303

The number of Fantasy Football League points Salah earned in 2017–18. It was the first time any player had broken the 300-point barrier.

102

Average number of minutes between Mo's Premier League goals for Chelsea and Liverpool, the best ever (10 goals or more.

At full speed, Mohamed Salah is almost unstoppable. He combines his blistering pace with great balance and a powerful shot.

2023

The year in which Mo Salah's renewed contract with Liverpool will come to an end.

MO'S MATES

Wherever he has played, Mo Salah has made friends on and off the field. His footballing partnerships with some of the game's great players have also brought out the best of them and him.

The sorcerer and his apprentice. Italian legend Francesco Totti quickly recognised the talent in Roma's young striker.

FRANCESCO TOTTI

"He's calm, great, very quiet and has such confidence about him," Salah said of the teammate who had been a childhood hero. "I learned a lot from him," he added. When Salah joined Roma, he was able to share the last two years of the Roma legend's 24-year career at the club and when Totti made his last ever appearance for Roma, it was Mo who had the honour of making way for him.

MOHAMED ABOUTRIKA

Before there was Salah, there was Mohamed Aboutrika. Known as "The Egyptian Zidane", he is regarded as the greatest African player never to play in Europe and is still idolized by many Egyptians, including Mo. In the short time their careers crossed they formed an often lethal partnership for the national team, especially in the 2012 Olympic Games and the 2014 World Cup qualifiers. Aboutrika retired from football in 2013, but remains a friend, role model and mentor to Salah.

EDIN DZEKO

The Bosnian striker joined Roma after a disappointing time at Manchester City, but continued to struggle in Italy. His second season, however, saw him reborn as the Salah effect kicked in. The two formed the most prolific strike partnership in Serie A, hitting 44 league goals between them. After Salah left, Dzeko continued to shine, but his season's goal haul dropped significantly. No wonder Dzeko missed the man he described as "a great player and a great guy".

At Roma, Edin Dzeko (right) and Mo Salah formed a deadly strike partnership which amassed 44 league goals in one season.

Sadio Mané (left) and Mo Salah combined to terrify many Premier League and European defences in 2017–18.

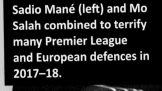

SADIO MANÉ

It's never easy arriving at a club as big as Liverpool as a record signing. Luckily, Mo had a fellow African in Sadio Mané to show him the ropes. The Senegalese international had already made his mark in his first season at Anfield, but when Salah joined him and Roberto Firmino up front they formed an electric and devastating trio. Sadio had such a great year, many fancied him to take the 2018 African Footballer of the Year, but he was beaten into second place by the man he calls his closest friend at the club.

MO-MANIA

Mo's incredible performances have turned Egyptians into Liverpool fans, inspired Scousers to sing Muslim-loving chants and seen millions worldwide become captivated with the Reds' striker.

"When we came out for training before the Manchester City tie," Jürgen Klopp quipped about the session before the UEFA Champions League quarter-final second leg, "I said, 'Come on everybody, let's go out naked because no-one will realize, they are just looking at Mo'." It was in April 2018 and we had still not hit peak Mo-Mania. There were still the Champions League run, the Golden Boot and other prestigious awards to come.

In Egypt, Salah's displays in the Africa Cup of Nations and the World Cup 2018 qualifiers had already made him a hero. With no previous affiliation to giant and fierce rival clubs Al Ahly or Zamalek, and careful to tread the political tightrope (a downfall of previous footballing heroes), he appealed to all fans. Streets were named in his honour, he was received by the country's President Abdul Fattah al-Sisi and fronted anti-drugs and anti-smoking campaigns aimed at young Egyptians.

His success in the Premier League, however, won him – and Liverpool – fans across the Middle East and Africa. After he won the PFA Player of the Year his name trended on Twitter across the region and, in the first year the African Footballer of the Year was decided by an online vote, Mo swept to victory. Saudi newspaper *Al-Watan* ran a headline: "The Pharaoh: Joy of 2017 and hope of 2018", dedicating nine pages to Salah in their New Year's Day edition, while authorities even decided to give him a piece of land in the Islamic holy city of Makkah (Mecca).

Back in the UK, his achievements and personality had earned Salah friends beyond Merseyside. The British Museum decided to display his adidas boots alongside the statues of ancient pharaohs. And, as newspaper back pages lauded the "Egyptian King", English football legends lined up to congratulate him on his PFA award, with Gary Lineker saying "he's been a breath of fresh air to our football" and Steven Gerrard tweeting: "Without a shadow of a doubt, he's the best player on the planet right now". Around the world many were nodding in agreement.

Mohamed Salah collects the 2017 African Footballer of the Year award in Accra, Ghana.

Liverpool fans find their own way to pay homage to their hero.

Salah's likeness can be found absolutely everywhere in Egypt.

More than any other team, Roma knew what to expect if Mo had a chance to score, but in the UEFA Champions League semi-final, they still couldn't stop him.

THE DEADLY RED

If signing Mo Salah from Roma was a gamble for Liverpool, it was one that came off in the most spectacular fashion as the striker had an unforgettable season.

Liverpool had tried and failed to sign Salah in 2014, but they had continued to watch his progress. They were not the only ones to be impressed with the Egyptian's improvement. "We played with Dortmund against him," said Reds boss Jürgen Klopp. "And it was 'what the …?'"

Some claimed Liverpool's £36.9 million record signing from Roma was a "gamble", but Klopp knew what he was adding to the squad. "One of those things is speed," he explained. "He brings that, as well as being able to provide

and to finish." Salah took the number 11 shirt (Roberto Firmino switched to No. 9) and marked his Liverpool league debut with a tap-in against Watford. Klopp later would claim it took him half an hour to settle to the Premier League. Liverpool fans agreed, voting him Player of the Month in August.

Mo never looked back. The "new" muscular and defensively aware Salah, combined with his pace and skill, were ideally suited to the Premier League. His link play with Firmino and Sadio

Mané seemed to develop instantly, but it was the unerring accuracy of his shooting that made the headlines. Often he found the net at the climax of a lethal counter-attack, but he also hit stunning curling shots from distance, exhibited incredible dribbling and super-calm finishing, pulled off surprise shots with little back-lift and used his close control in the penalty area to give him a half-second to execute a deadly accurate strike.

As the season drew to a close, Liverpool had one eye on their Champions League run and another on a top-four finish. Salah's battle with Harry Kane for the Golden Boot was a side issue – but a compelling one. As Kane suffered an injury, Mo's four goals in a 5–0 thrashing of Watford put him ahead in the race. He never let up; netting another four in the last seven games, he took his total to 32 – a Premier League record. Added to Mo's

10 assists and the Premier League, Professional Footballers' Association and Football Writers' Association Player of the Year awards, it amounted to one incredible debut season. Some gamble!

Salah immediately settled into Premier League football with superb performances and clinical finishing.

The link up play between Salah and his teammates – especially Roberto Firmino (right) and Sadio Mané – led to some breathtaking moves.

KING OF THE KOP

Liverpool fans' affection for their "Egyptian King" knows no bounds and they celebrate their hero as only they can, in the songs of the world famous Kop.

The Kop found a new hero in Salah and they wasted no time in letting him know…

Liverpool's Kop may be famous for their "You'll Never Walk Alone" anthem, but at times in the 2017–18 season you could have been forgiven for thinking it had been jettisoned for another song. On countless occasions you could hear the refrain: "Mo Salah, Mo Salah, Mo Salah… Running down the wing… Salah-ah-ah-ah-ah-ah-ah… Egyptian King!" sung to the tune of James' 1989 classic "Sit Down".

Of course, Mo loves the song. He says it inspires him to play better and that the other players even sing it in the changing room. It is part of that special Anfield atmosphere and one of the reasons he joined the Reds. He had witnessed it

as part of the 2014 Chelsea team and vowed to play for them one day. After all, even as a child 4,000 miles away, watching the Premier League on TV, Liverpool were always his favourite club.

Any supporter is going to love a player who scores 44 goals in his first season. But Salah has established a deep connection with the Liverpool faithful. As much as his breathtaking skills, direct style and work-rate, they have fallen for his humble goal celebrations, the way he plays the game with a smile and for the off-the-field modest guy with a great sense of humour. That's why they chant his name, wear "Salah" replica shirts in their thousands – and even don Mo wigs

WHY HAVE A L.F.C. CHICKEN KIEV WHEN WE GOT TIKKA MO SALAH 96

...And honouring him with that famous Scouse humour.

in the style of their hero's shaggy afro. After being voted the Liverpool Player of the Month by fans in his first two months at the club, he followed it up with another five wins– and predictably, he walked off with the fans' Player of the Season too.

Meanwhile, the Kop's love for their new hero was emerging in more chants. One in particular became newsworthy around the world. Using Dodgy's 1996 hit "Good Enough" they dared suggest: "If he's good enough for you, he's good enough for me. If he scores another few, then I'll be Muslim too." Some wondered if Mo might be offended, but he translated and tweeted it to his Arab followers along with three heart-eye emojis. The man is a Liverpool legend – already!

For his part Mo made it clear he enjoyed the songs and was loving every minute at Anfield.

2017 AFRICA CUP OF NATIONS

Mo Salah had been instrumental in getting Egypt to the 2017 Africa Cup of Nations and coach Héctor Cúper was relying on him to inspire the team to glory in Gabon.

Cúper's cautious game plan was soon pretty clear: keep a clean sheet and hope that Salah, the star of the well-organized side, could create something special. It failed in the first game, a goalless stalemate with Mali, and the second match, against Uganda, appeared to be going the same way.

Then, in the 88th minute, Mo shaped for his signature curling shot, but held back and, instead, fed the overlapping substitute Abdellah Said, who drilled home the winner. In the final group game, against leaders Ghana, it was Salah who scored the only goal – in the 11th minute – blasting home a perfectly placed free-kick from 20 yards. Solid defending for the final 80-odd minutes meant Egypt reached the knock-out stages as Group D winners.

Despite Mo Salah's best efforts, all saved by an alert keeper, the quarter-final against Morocco was another tight affair until another late goal – a scrambled effort after a corner, again scored by a substitute, Kahraba – sent the Pharaohs into the last four. Salah was proving to be a real star of the tournament – a status reinforced when his sublime chip put the Pharaohs 1–0 up in the 66th minute of the semi-final against Burkino Faso. The underdogs however equalized seven minutes later and took the game to extra time and then penalties. Mo coolly slotted his spot-kick inside the foot of the right post, but it was veteran keeper Essam El-Hadary who proved the real hero with two spot-kick saves.

The jubilant Egyptians who packed the streets of Cairo after every victory had even more to cheer when Salah cleverly played in Mohamed Elneny to put Egypt ahead in the final against Cameroon. This time, however, their plan to soak up the pressure backfired as Cameroon equalized and grabbed the winner with just minutes to spare.

The Egyptian players and fans were dejected, but they had shown they had a team with heart and a player capable of winning any match. Salah, named in the Team of the Tournament, had not only been a goal threat but he was also at the centre of every attacking move. The World Cup in Russia could not come soon enough...

Mohamed Salah celebrates with teammates after scoring in the 2017 Africa Cup of Nations semi-final against Burkina Faso.

Mo in control in the Africa Cup of Nations final. The Pharoahs would eventually be stunned by a late Cameroon winner.

Egyptian joy after Salah's strike against Ghana sent Egypt to the top of their Africa Cup of Nations group.

GREAT LIVERPOOL GOALS

From the moment Mo pulled on that Liverpool shirt he just couldn't stop scoring. They came from all distances and directions, but these are some of the best...

LIVERPOOL V ROMA
(Champions League semi-final)
24 April 2018

As Mo helped the Reds take Roma apart it's hard to decide which of his two goals was better. Both were textbook Magic Mo: the first, a clipped shot from just inside the penalty area that curled into the goal so perfectly that it kissed the underside of the crossbar; the second was a darting run which ended with an impudent chip over the advancing keeper. Of course, in true modest style, his muted celebrations showed Mo's respect for his former club.

Technique, application and pure class as Mohamed Salah curls home a brilliant effort to begin the UEFA Champions League rout against Roma.

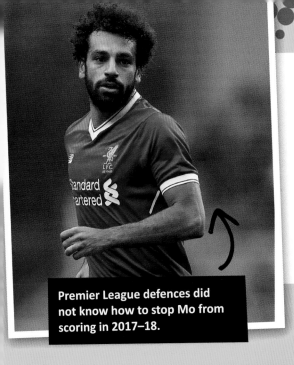

Premier League defences did not know how to stop Mo from scoring in 2017–18.

LIVERPOOL V TOTTENHAM HOTSPUR
(Premier League)
4 February 2018

"The only other man who can score that goal is Messi," said Sky Sports pundit Jamie Carragher. Deep into injury time, Salah, who had already scored once and tormented the Tottenham defence all game long, jinked his way past three defenders inside Spurs' penalty area. He was still left with the tightest of spaces, but kept his cool and his balance to poke the ball past goalkeeper Hugo Lloris.

LIVERPOOL V BOURNEMOUTH
(Premier League)
14 April 2018

Standing at just 5 ft 9 inches (1.75m), Salah's headed goals are collector's items. And this is definitely one to remember. Trent Alexander-Arnold sent in a diagonal cross from the right touchline 40 yards away. Mo, unable to look at both the ball and the goal, relied on instinct and skill to flick an exquisite header over the outstretched hand of keeper Asmir Begovic. It was Mo's 30th league goal of the season – the first player in Europe to reach that milestone.

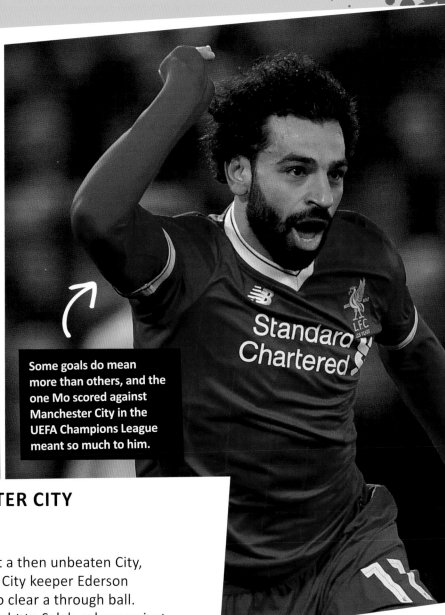

Some goals do mean more than others, and the one Mo scored against Manchester City in the UEFA Champions League meant so much to him.

LIVERPOOL V MANCHESTER CITY
(Premier League)
14 January 2018

Of the four goals Liverpool put past a then unbeaten City, Salah's was the most breathtaking. City keeper Ederson had raced out of his penalty area to clear a through ball. Unfortunately for him, it went straight to Salah, who was just inside the City half. But this was no "hit and hope" response. Mo controlled the ball, moved forward and then curled it back over the goalkeeper into an empty net from 40 yards out.

FROM TRIUMPH TO TEARS – CHAMPIONS LEAGUE 2018

Mo Salah was unstoppable throughout Liverpool's UEFA Champions League adventure – only to suffer heartbreak and agony in the final.

It's all smiles as teammates run to congratulate Mo after his cheekiest of finishes against Porto in the round-of-16.

Mo had played Champions League football before. His goals for Basel against Chelsea had brought him to the attention of Europe's elite and he was part of Roma's spirited run to the last 16 in 2016–17, but this was Liverpool – a team with far greater European pedigree.

In the group stage, Liverpool sent out a message of intent, scoring 23 goals in their six matches. Mo scored five of these, the pick of them being dispatched after a drag-back near the penalty spot had left three Spartak Moscow defenders on the ground. In the 5–0 thrashing of Porto in the first leg of the round-of-16 match, while Sadio Mané hit a hat-trick, Salah's goal was mesmerizing as he played keepy-uppy around a defender and the keeper. Qualification for the quarter-final was a formality but Liverpool drew Manchester City, whose form in the Premier League was imperious.

Salah only played 52 minutes of the first leg, but by then the damage had been done. Liverpool were 3–0 up after their press and counter-attacking had completely stunned City. Mo provided the cutting

No celebrations, just tears as a distraught Mo Salah realises he will play no further part in the final.

Real Madrid's Cristiano Ronaldo, who was injured early in the Euro 2016 final, is one of the first to console Mo as he exits the Champions League final.

edge with a sharply taken goal and a cross which Roberto Firmino headed home. In the second leg, he finished the job when keeper Ederson could only palm away the ball from Sadio Mané and Mo collected the loose ball before chipping home. There was no way back for the league leaders.

Mo put sentiment aside as his old friends Roma visited in the semi-final. It was a Salah masterclass as he calmed Liverpool nerves with a trademark curler into the top corner, delicately chipped the keeper in a one-on-one for the second, set up Mané for a third, then squared for Firmino to add a fourth.

Only when he was taken off did Roma fight back, but Liverpool had done enough.

The mouth-watering final matched Liverpool with Real Madrid. It was billed as Ronaldo versus Salah. Could the Egyptian overshadow the world's greatest player? We were denied the opportunity to find out as, after just 30 minutes, Mo suffered an agonizing shoulder injury after tussling with Real's Sergio Ramos and falling awkwardly. He left the field in tears, his fans around the world were shocked, frustrated and some angry with the defender. The Salah-less Liverpool slumped to a disappointing defeat.

MO SALAH – A COACH'S DREAM

With a natural born talent, an eagerness to learn and a willingness to put in hard hours at the training ground, Mo Salah is a delight to coach. He is also lucky enough to have had coaches with the patience and insight to help him become one of the game's greats.

"Then there's the job Klopp has done. I tried all year to get him to play more centrally and he kept going wide to get the ball. It seems to me he now understands what his starting position has to be and is drawing great benefit from it."
Luciano Spalletti, Salah's second coach at Roma, on Mo's improvement at Liverpool

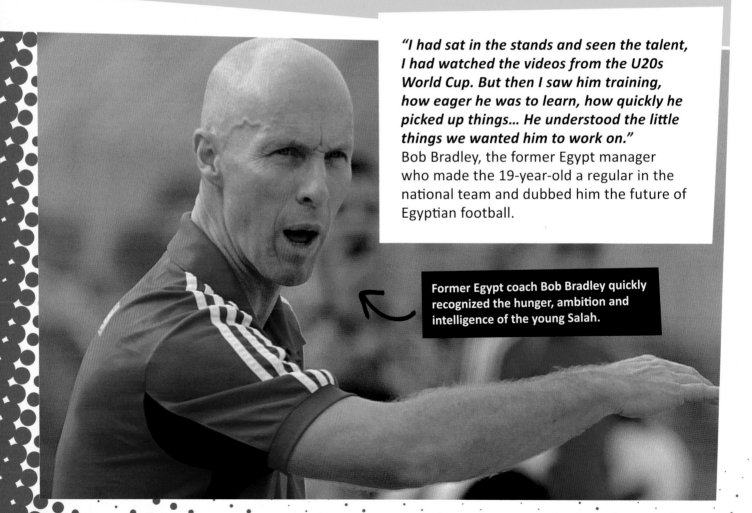

"I had sat in the stands and seen the talent, I had watched the videos from the U20s World Cup. But then I saw him training, how eager he was to learn, how quickly he picked up things… He understood the little things we wanted him to work on."
Bob Bradley, the former Egypt manager who made the 19-year-old a regular in the national team and dubbed him the future of Egyptian football.

Former Egypt coach Bob Bradley quickly recognized the hunger, ambition and intelligence of the young Salah.

"The last player I know who had the same influence on a team performance was Diego Maradona. The boys love playing together with him, he loves playing with them."
Jürgen Klopp

Liverpool boss Jürgen Klopp has got the best from his star striker and the pair have developed a special relationship.

"He is young enough and has enough potential to improve... There is still work to do and I'm really happy about that. But what he is, in his mind, he is a real goal-getter and that's cool."
Klopp again

"Mohamed was willing to sacrifice everything."
Hamdi Nooh, who gave the 17-year-old Salah his debut at El Mokawloon

"He's quick and technical. They're important attributes to make the difference in modern football."
Rudi Garcia, coach at Roma when Salah arrived

"He is strong mentally and has the focus on football. He is not interested in everything else."
Murat Yakin, coach at Basel, who concentrated on improving the striker's finishing

"Perhaps only Leo Messi is quicker than him with the ball at his feet."
Vincenzo Montella, Mo's coach at Fiorentina

Former FC Basel and current Grasshopper Zurich manager Murat Yakin, who helped Mo adapt to European football.

GLOBAL SUPERSTAR

Mohamed Salah has made such an impact around the world that his name and image are now recognized beyond the sphere of football, a sure sign that he is a true superstar.

"I do not go to bed at night, thinking: 'Wow, how good is Salah?'" Liverpool boss Jürgen Klopp said in 2018. There are, however, an increasing number of football fans around the world who do just that. The Egyptian's performances for Roma, Liverpool and his country alerted the world to a new talent ready to join the elite of world football.

Mo's growing global popularity has already put him in the "superstar" bracket. He has more than ten million followers on Facebook, 18 million in Instagram and six million on Twitter, he has sponsorship deals with global brands like DHL, Vodaphone and Adidas ("I wear these for 100 million Egyptians," he tweeted with a photo of his special blue World Cup boots) and, having been named the Premier League Player of the Season, was featured as one of the top players appearing at the 2018 World Cup.

The key to Mo's popularity is that although he is a superstar he doesn't act like one. The only arrogance fans see in him are his impudent skills. Off the pitch, his down-to-earth and modest personality wins Mo friends among even his teams' fiercest rivals. The work he puts in for the team, defensively and bringing players into the game, also earns admiration from fans and teammates. "There's no danger of him getting carried away," said Liverpool goalkeeper Simon Mignolet. "He's very focused on his job."

The really great players inspire their teams to greatness. Mo's heroics have already helped Liverpool to a Champions League Final and his team to the World Cup finals. Héctor Cúper, Egypt's manager in Russia, has already admitted: "Salah's importance to us is like Messi's importance to Argentina," but Mo's game is still developing and at 26, he is already showing leadership qualities at club and international level.

Salah is already being spoken of in the same breath as Cristiano Ronaldo and Lionel Messi and as those players enter the twilight of their playing careers, there is every chance that Mo could be talked about as the world's greatest player in the near future. Can he maintain, or even improve upon the amazing form of the 2017–18 season? Many players, experts and fans seem pretty convinced that he can...

At his request the plane to take Egypt's team to the 2018 FIFA World Cup in Russia was repainted without Mo as the main focus.

Mo Salah's boots now sit alongside other Egyptian treasures, such as the statues of Pharaohs and the Rosetta Stone, in the British Museum.

Even in America! US artist Brandan "Bmike" Odums' mural of Mo Salah on display in New York's Time Square. Mo tweeted a picture of it which quickly went viral on social media.

GREAT EGYPT GOALS

He is the talisman of the national team. Scoring at a rate better than a goal every other game, Mo's goals have turned Egypt into a footballing force. Here are some of his most memorable...

Salah's sizzling strike is on the rise, passing the Ghanaian wall and heading for the net.

EGYPT V GHANA,
Africa Cup of Nations,
25 January 2017

In a tight African Cup of Nations Group D match, goals were always going to be at a premium, so Mo's 22nd-minute free-kick was invaluable. And what a strike! From 20 yards out, he hit a blistering but perfectly controlled shot. It passes the edge of the Ghana wall at knee height but rises to almost burst the top of the inside netting.

Mo's 2013 hat-trick against Zimbabwe included one of his now trademark runs and deft finishes. A star was born.

EGYPT V ZIMBABWE,
FIFA World Cup 2014 qualifier,
9 June 2013

Salah truly announced himself in international football with a hat-trick in Harare. The second goal was the pick of them. Mo received a pass from his hero Mohamed Aboutrika just inside the opposition half. His first touch sent the ball through the legs of the last defender, he took the long route round him, but sped into the penalty area, before effortlessly clipping the ball past the keeper. A star was born.

Egypt fans dubbed The Pharaohs the "Pass to Salah" team and when Kahraba did just that against Burkino Faso, Mo did the rest and Egypt had one foot in the final.

EGYPT V BURKINO FASO,
Africa Cup of Nations,
1 February 2017

Egypt were on the back foot for more than an hour of this semi-final before a touch of pure class put them on top. A fine team move saw a flurry of first-time passes end with a cross to Kahraba's feet. He carefully laid it back to the edge of the penalty area, where Mo hit the most elegant and precise side-footer into the top left corner. Sumptuous.

EGYPT V NIGER,
Africa Cup of Nations 2012 qualifier,
8 October 2011

The 19-year-old Salah, playing in just his second international, picked up the ball halfway inside the Niger half, dummied to take the ball down the line but, instead, nutmegged an opponent and knocked the ball square to Mohamed Elneny. Mo then motored diagonally into the penalty area, where his good friend and El Mokawloon teammate gently played the ball into his path. A Salah side-foot finished the move for his first goal for the Pharaohs and it's a beauty!

MO SALAH – RECORD BREAKER

As his goal-scoring spree continued unabated, Mo Salah's astonishing 2017–18 season saw records tumbling across the board.

PREMIER LEAGUE RECORDS

32
Most goals in a 38-game Premier League season

3
Most Premier League Player of the Month awards in one season (November, February and March)

24
Most Premier League games scored in a single season

3
Premier League teams out-scored by a single player in one season (Huddersfield Town, Swansea City and West Bromwich Albion)

17
Most teams scored against in a Premier Leagu season: (shared with Ian Wright and Robin van Persie)

32
Highest-scoring Egyptian in Premier League history

32
Highest-scoring African in a Premier League season

25
Most left-footed goals in one Premier League season

The Football Writers' Association Player of the Year award capped a remarkable season for Mo.

LIVERPOOL FC RECORDS

32
The most goals in any Premier League season for Liverpool

32
The most goals in a debut season for the club

11
First Liverpool player to hit double figures in a Champions League campaign (teammate Roberto Firmino equalled the record in the same game!)

It was a Premier League season of smiles for Salah as the goals just kept coming.

32
Fewest games to reach 25 goals in a season (for more than a century)

7
Most LFC Player of the Month awards in a season

MO SALAH AT THE 2018 FIFA WORLD CUP

The 2018 FIFA World Cup was an unhappy tournament not just for Mo Salah, but for all of Egypt. He had faced a race against time to be fit even to take part in the tournament, but he did leave it with two more goals to his name.

With Mo's scintillating form for Liverpool and a favourable draw, there were high hopes for the Pharaohs in their first World Cup finals since 1990. All those dreams were wrecked in the UEFA Champions League Final when Mo suffered a dislocated shoulder and, with just 20 days remaining until Egypt's first game in Russia, there was much doubt that their talisman would be fit to play at all.

It certainly was problematic that Salah could not train with his teammates. Nevertheless, on the eve of the Pharaohs' first match, against Uruguay, coach Héctor Cúper stated, "I can almost assure you 100 per cent he will play." The key word was "almost", as Mo didn't start and, in fact, didn't feature at all as Egypt fell to a heart-breaking last-minute 1–0 defeat.

Four days later, in St Petersburg, Mo was in the starting line-up against Russia. Clearly not fully fit, Salah still created chances, including a dangerous shot on the turn from 18 yards. The hosts were already 3–0 up when a run from Mo was halted inside the penalty area; the decision was reviewed by VAR and judged to be a foul inside the area. Salah coolly dispatched the penalty to become only the third Egyptian player to score at a World Cup.

Despite Mo's efforts, the match ended 3–1 to Russia and Egypt, with a game to go, could not

Mo finally got to taste World Cup action in Egypt's second game against host nation, Russia.

qualify for the knock-out stages. At least, in their final match against Saudi Arabia, Mo was able to leave his mark on the tournament with a classic Salah strike.

Outsprinting the defence, he brought down a dropping long downfield pass with an exquisite touch. Still at full speed and with the Saudi goalkeeper racing off his line on a collision course, Mo executed a perfectly weighted lob into the net to give the Pharaohs the lead. For all of the goal's great quality, with Egypt's hopes of advancement over, there really wasn't much in the way of celebration.

Despite being less than fully fit, Mo had shown glimpses of the player the world had wanted to see. He had been his country's best player and scored both their goals, but Egypt went home wondering what might have been.

Mo Salah in action against Saudi Arabia in Egypt's third and final match. Despite a lack of fitness, he still showed some moments of magic.

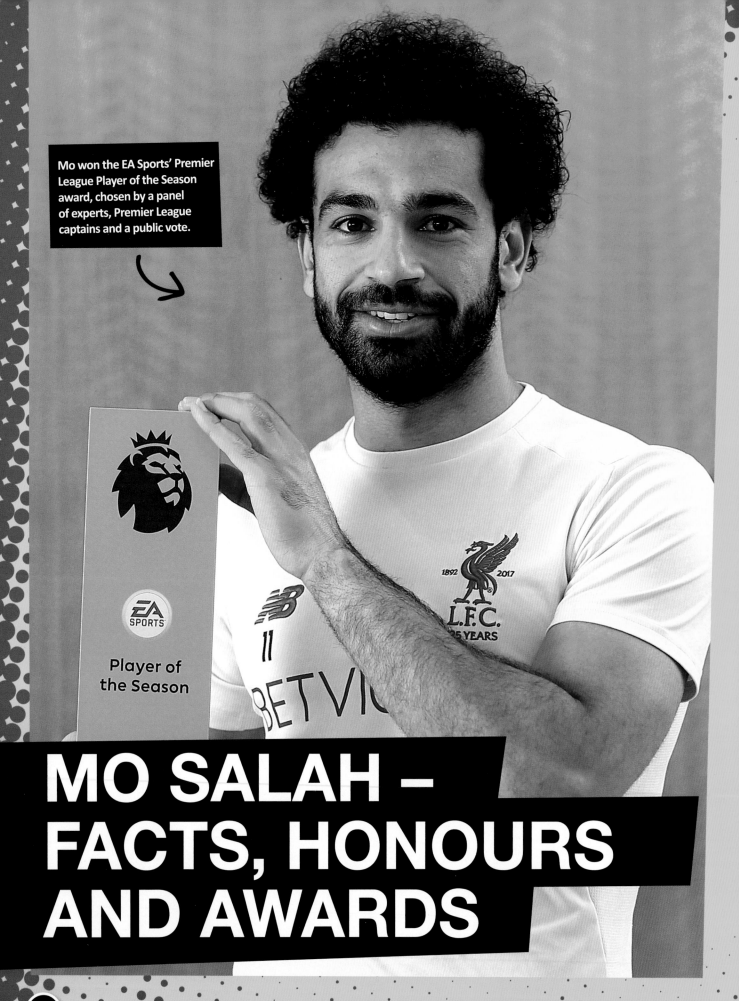

Mo won the EA Sports' Premier League Player of the Season award, chosen by a panel of experts, Premier League captains and a public vote.

Player of the Season

MO SALAH –
FACTS, HONOURS
AND AWARDS

Birth Date: 15 June 1992
Birth Place: Nagrig, Egypt
Height: 1.75m (5ft 9in)
Weight: 159 lbs (72 kg)

Total League Appearances: 215
Total League Goals: 89
International Record: 59 Appearances, 33 Goals

TEAM HONOURS

Basel
Swiss Super League: 2012–13
Swiss Cup runner-up: 2012–13

Liverpool
UEFA Champions League runner-up: 2017–18

Egypt U20
African Youth Championship third place: 2011

Egypt
Africa Cup of Nations runner-up: 2017

INDIVIDUAL AWARDS

CAF Most Promising Talent of the Year: 2012
UAFA Golden Boy (Most Promising European-based Under-21 player): 2012
SAFP (Swiss) Golden Player: 2013
El Heddaf Arab Footballer of the Year: 2013, 2017
A.S. Roma Player of the Season: 2015–16
Globe Soccer Best Arab Player of the Year: 2016
CAF Team of the Year: 2016, 2017
CAF Africa Cup of Nations Team of the Tournament: 2017
Premier League Player of the Month: November 2017, February 2018, March 2018
PFA Player of the Month: November 2017, December 2017, February 2018, March 2018

African Footballer of the Year: 2017
BBC African Footballer of the Year: 2017
Goal's Arab Player of the Year: 2017
PFA Players' Player of the Year: 2017–18
FWA Footballer of the Year: 2017–18
EA Sports Premier League Player of the Season: 2017–18
Premier League Golden Boot: 2017–18
Premier League Player of the Season: 2017–18
PFA Team of the Year: 2017–18 Premier League
Liverpool F.C. Fans Player of the Year: 2017–18
Liverpool F.C. Players' Player of the Year: 2017–18
PFA Fans' Player of the Year: 2017–18
UEFA Champions League Squad of the Season: 2017–18

Mo with the PFA Player of the Year Award voted by his fellow professionals. He also won BBC Sport's online award, polling 76% of votes.

WHAT'S NEXT FOR MOHAMED SALAH?

We have seen brilliant performances from the phenomenal Egyptian for Roma, Liverpool and his national team, but there is plenty more on Mo's to-do list...

It may seem greedy to ask from more from a player who has lit up the Premier League in his first season, but everyone who has seen Salah play realises he could be the world's best. "Mo played a fantastic season but Cristiano [Ronaldo] has played 15 seasons like this," said Liverpool boss Jürgen Klopp. "If Mo can do that, we will see. He has fantastic potential. The next few seasons will show if he can do something similar."

Despite being named African Player of the Year, Mo did not even feature among the 30 nominees for the 2017 Ballon d'Or, the award for the world's greatest player. He will surely make the 2018 list and with a great start to the 2018–19 season, could even challenge Messi, Ronaldo and Neymar for the ultimate prize.

First, he must recover from the disappointment of Egypt's 2018 World Cup performance. Hopefully the Pharaohs can learn from their experience, come back stronger and enable Mo to shine on the international stage. Their sights will be set on the 2019 Africa Cup of Nations in Cameroon and then the World Cup finals in Qatar in 2022. If so, a 30-year-old Salah at his peak could well surpass Hossam Hassan's Egyptian record of 70 goals (although Ahmed Hassan's record 184 appearances might still be unassailable).

Back in the Premier League, Liverpool have a squad that can challenge for domestic silverware in the years ahead and, in Mo Salah, a match-winner and big-game player. He is capable of inspiring the Reds to the league title and even personally beating Ian Rush's 1983–84 record of 47 goals in a season. And, of course, there is unfinished business – the chance to make amends for the disappointment of the 2018 UEFA Champions League Final.

The standards Mo has set at Liverpool are difficult to exceed; he is a joy to watch and the complete player. Fans also know he will do all he can to raise his game even higher. He has the world at his feet and they await the day when "The Egyptian King" conquers the world.

Salah will be carrying the hopes of the nation again as Egypt attempt to win the 2019 Africa Cup of Nations.

Clearly in the same class as Cristiano Ronaldo, the Ballon d'Or is now in Mo's sights.

QUIZ

How much do you know about Mo? These questions will test your knowledge of the Liverpool and Egypt superstar.

1 Which current Arsenal player played with Mo at El Mokawloon and Basel?
a) Pierre-Emerick Aubameyang.
b) Mohamed Elneny. c) Shkodran Mustafi.

2 What was the transfer fee (in Euros) paid by Basel to El Mokawloon for Mo Salah?
a) €2.5 million. b) €3.5 million.
c) €5.5million.

3 Who did Mo replace as the Liverpool number 11?
a) Luis Suárez. b) Daniel Sturridge.
c) Roberto Firmino.

4 Against which of his former clubs did Mo Salah receive his first and only ever red card?
a) Chelsea. b) Basel. c) Fiorentina.

5 Who did Mo score four goals against in a Premier League game in March 2018?
a) Watford. b) Tottenham Hotspur.
c) West Bromwich Albion.

6 Which of these players was one of Mo's childhood football heroes?
a) Wayne Rooney. b) Thierry Henry.
c) Zinedine Zidane.

7 How many UEFA Champions League goals does Salah have in his career?
a) 11. b) 13. c) 17.

8 Against which nation did Mo play his first World Cup finals match?
a) Uruguay. b) Russia. c) Saudi Arabia.

9 Salah scored his first Roma goal against which Serie A club?
a) Fiorentina. b) Juventus. c) Sassuaolo.

10 Against which club did Salah make his Premier League debut for Chelsea?
a) Newcastle United. b) Watford. c) Everton.

11 In which year did Salah make his debut for Egypt's senior national team?
a) 2010. b) 2011. c) 2012.

12 At what age did Salah make his professional debut?
a) 17. b) 18. c) 19.

13 What was the transfer fee (in euros) paid by Liverpool to Roma for Mo Salah?
a) €20 million. b) €31 million. c) €42 million.

14 How many Premier League goals did Mo score in 2017–18?
a) 30. b) 31. c) 32.

15 To which club did Chelsea loan Salah in 2015?
a) Roma. b) Basel. c) Fiorentina.

16 Mo's daughter shares the name of which holy site?
a) Kaaba. b) Makkah. c) Medina.

17 How many assists did Mo provide for Liverpool in the Premier League in 2017–18?
a) 6. b) 8. c) 10.

18 From group stage to final, how many goals did Mo score on Liverpool's route to the 2018 Champions League Final?
a) 5. b) 10. c) 12.

19 In which year did Mo play in the Olympic Games?
a) 2016. b) 2012. c) 2008.

20 What number did Salah choose to wear at Fiorentina?
a) 10. b) 47. c) 74.

ANSWERS 1 b (Mohamed Elneny) **2 a** (€2.5 million).
3 c (Roberto Firmino). **4 c** (Fiorentina). **5 a** (Watford).
6 c (Zinedine Zidane). **7 a** (11). **8 b** (Russia).
9 c (Sassuaolo). **10 a** (Newcastle United). **11 b** (2011).
12 a (17). **13 c** (€42 million). **14 c** (2). **15 c** (Fiorentina).
16 b (Makkah). **17 c** (10). **18 b** (10). **19 b** (2012).
20 c (74).